# SN
# Everythin

# to get Started on Snapchat

## (or, How to Use Snapchat Like a Teen)

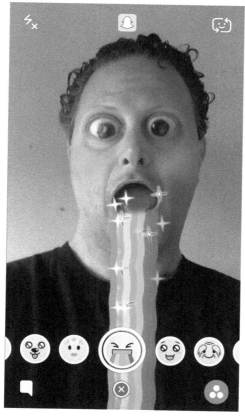

**Scott Perry**

**Sperry Media**

**Santa Monica, CA**

First Edition: July 2016
Published by Sperry Media

Contact the author for bulk purchases, as well as speaking engagements / consulting at http://www.howtosnapchatbook.com

# CONTENTS

# PREFACE

I am not a teenager, nor do I play one on TV.

I am 45 years old, and have made a career of explaining emerging social platforms to entertainment firms, startups, and Fortune 500 companies.

I've been on Social Media since the Friendster days, painfully endured MySpace (apologies to friends who worked there but the UI made my eyes scream), and was one of the first adults on Facebook post-.edu.

I was on Twitter from the 40404 days (and had my first username, @alroker, unceremoniously stripped away when they started verifying identities).

I stumbled through Tumblr, flew through flickr, and freaked out when I was late to the party on Instagram (oh no, user number 400,000! I think they're somewhere past 500 million users now).

And being an old man (ha), I love the short / long-form text formats of Medium and Quora as a way to express ideas and share knowledge.

But Snapchat is different.

I was hipped to the service years ago by a friend's kids.

And I'll be the first to admit, I didn't get it.

Back then, you sent a still pic, friends pressed down to look at it for like 5 seconds, then it disappeared forever. All one-on-one, no broadcast capabilities, nothing else to it.

And since the success of your experience is based on the quality of your network -- it was kind of hard to find my adult friends on the service, and I was not about to befriend a bunch of teenagers in order to send disappearing pictures -- I let it go after a couple tries. Poof.

But over the years, Snapchat has added a ton more features that allow multiple forms of communication -- users can now send text, audio, video chats and messages, save Snaps into Memories, and even view Stories from friends and brand-name publishers.

Not only that, the size of Snapchat's base has grown so large and active, that it has become impossible for adults to ignore.

I constantly hear among adults, "Yeah, Snapchat? That's where I draw the line, I give up!"

But if you have children, work with Millennials, or need to keep up with tech trends, then knowing how to use Snapchat is extremely important, especially as Snapchat grows beyond its massive base, and as other platforms attempt to co-opt Snapchat's better features.

You may be happy just using SMS to text pictures to friends or posting cute content onto Facebook, and that's totally fine.

And I'll be the first to admit, even though Snapchat does have a Support section, it can feel like you're flying without a net.

Using Snapchat is like playing a video game, in which the more you play, the more you learn tips & tricks to make for a better experience.

I've made a living translating tech talk into proper English, so that busy adults can easily learn this stuff in a short amount of time.

I get straight to the point on the most essential info that you need to get familiar and started on Snapchat.

With this handbook, you can go through all the basics of Snapchat in under an hour, and with a little bit of practice, be a pro in no time.

So fire up your mobile device and get ready -- Happy Snapping!

Scott Perry, author

PS, it's not necessary, but it does help to have a friend join at the same time, so you can immediately put all these tips into practice, and learn from each other along the way.

To that end, a special thanks to my friends Serena Ehrlich and Bryan Landers, who let me be bomb them with really bad face swaps and sample chats while building out this book.

# Once you have finished this book, stay on top of new features and trends by subscribing to our email list at

## HOWTOSNAPCHATBOOK.COM

# 1. A BRIEF HISTORY OF SNAPCHAT

Snapchat is a mobile communication platform, an ephemeral messaging service in which your any of your unsaved posts disappear after a set amount of time.

Snapchat is a great way to capture and share a moment, in a way that's more fun than just sending a picture or text.

Not only can you send a Snap to your friends, but you can layer Text, Doodles, and emoji Stickers on top of your picture or video.

Snapchat was created by Evan Spiegel and Bobby Murphy in 2011.

Its premise was simple; you took a still picture -- a **SNAP** -- and then sent it privately to friends, who could only view the picture for a set amount of time (only a few seconds) when the recipient held their thumb on the screen.

According to legend, the app experienced its first burst of fame while being shared at an Orange County (California) high school, which goes a long way to explaining its large, younger initial base.

Over the years, the app's growth trajectory and valuation in investment circles have made adults take note, but the addition of new features has made it a hit amongst teens and Millennials:

In 2012, Snapchat added video Snaps.

In 2013, Snapchat introduced Stories, which allows users to stitch together Snaps into a chronicle of their past 24 hours.

In 2014, Snapchat introduced Live, which curates big / local news from users' public Snaps. Geofilters also slowly rolled out.

In 2015, Snapchat launched Discover, in which publishing partners such as CNN, Vice, Cosmopolitan, and National Geographic build stories for Snapchat users to enjoy.

But it was that fateful day of December 15, 2015, as a 40 year old man got stuck on a jet ski, when adults really take note.

That 40 year old man, DJ Khaled, has shown that adults can use Snapchat to connect with friends, show the day-to-day minutiae of life, build a mass audience, tell a story, and most importantly, promote oneself, become a Brand, and get Sponsors. [more info on the business of Snapchat: http://bit.ly/snapbloom]

DJ Khaled's messages of inspiration draw millennials to his Stories, and his unique phraseology has become part of the Snapchat canon.

More than anything, DJ Khaled's Stories show that you can use the tools provided by Snapchat to tell your own narrative, and has since drawn more serious-minded adults to share knowledge in a way that no other platform can.

In July 2016, Snapchat added Memories as a way for users to save their Snaps in-app, thus enabling an even broader use of the app.

Snapchat has its own rules, its own cadence, its own code that can be very frustrating for the uninitiated to understand.

Hopefully this book will make it very easy for you to understand the basics of using Snapchat, and from there you can decide how deep you want to go -- whether it be to understand just what the hell your kids are doing, or building the foundation for world domination.

**But just understand this, you can only really do three things on Snapchat: Snap, Chat, and view Stories. How deep you get into any of this is up to you.**

Snapchat continues to add features at a rapid pace, and makes constant tweaks to the platform in order to appease users and boost engagement, so we'll keep adding more info in future editions of this book, as well as on our site **HOWTOSNAPCHATBOOK.COM**.

## So let's get you one step closer to hopping on board with a brief overview the basics.

# 2. SNAPCHAT FAQs

**Normally, Frequently Asked Questions are buried in the back of the book -- you can skip this chapter and come back later if you like, but I figured we'd put this up front so you know what to expect.**

Do not be discouraged by the tons of info being thrown around in this section; a lot of this will make more sense once you have actually played around with the app.

## WHAT IS SNAPCHAT?
Snapchat is an multi-media, mostly image-based, ephemeral messaging service. Your private Snaps disappear after your friend has viewed it; your public Stories disappear after 24 hours.

This handbook focuses on the basics you need to understand Snapchat in its simplest form -- how far you go down the rabbit hole is your choice.

## WHY DO I HAVE TO BE ON SNAPCHAT?
Because Snapchat's user base is HUGE, plain and simple.

The numbers are changing quickly, but by all measures (10 BILLION Daily Video Views, 150 Million Daily Active Users, 10,000 Photos Shared Per SECOND), Snapchat's user base is massive -- so big that it is only a matter of time that Snapchat becomes the second-largest social network / messaging service, only behind Facebook and WhatsApp.

If your life or your business involves Millennials or teens, you need to understand their preferred method of communication. You don't have to act like a kid and make silly faces covered in emojis while making Snaps, but it never hurts to have some fun as you learn.

And even though the platform may not be native to your peer group, it really is a fun way to communicate with others, both privately and publicly.

Adults are starting to adopt Snapchat as a communications medium, as "traditional" business people are using the platform to connect with clients and drive new business.

A lot of your younger competitors are already using Snapchat to showcase their hustle, and are building a significant base of followers. They're not just selling the cake, they're showing how the cake is made, where they get the ingredients, and involve their viewers in the process.

You don't have to use it as a business tool, but it is an option.

## WHY IS SOMETHING SO SIMPLE SO COMPLEX?
Honestly, with Snapchat, you can only really do three things:

**SNAP** a picture or video, then send privately to friends via Chat, or publicly to followers via your Story

**CHAT** with friends, using Text, Images, Doodles, Stickers, Voice, and Video

**WATCH** what others have posted as a public Story

The real complexity comes as you decide which tools you want to use to express yourself.

## SNAPS, CHATS, STORIES, DISCOVER, WTF?
A **SNAP** is a single picture or video that you take, and enhance with Stickers, Doodles, Filters, or Text

A **CHAT** is a private conversation between you and your friend(s)

A **STORY** is a series of Snaps you have posted for friends & followers to see publicly

**DISCOVER** is where you see friends' Stories, as well as Stories from partner channels

## EMOJI STICKERS, DOODLES, FILTERS, WTF?
These are the tools Snapchatters use to express themselves; it is the social visual language of a mobile-first generation, especially as screen sizes get smaller.

All this stuff -- Snaps, Chats, Stories, Discover, Stickers, Doodles, Filters, and more -- are all easily explained in Chapter 3 of this book.

## BUT I WANNA FACESWAP FACESWAP FACESWAP RIGHT NOW!!!
Patience Obi-Wan, we'll get to that too.

## WHO CAN SEE MY SNAPS, AND FOR HOW LONG?

When you make a Snap, Snapchat offers you two options -- you can either send that Snap directly to a friend (or friends) via **CHAT**, or you can post that Snap publicly to your **STORY**. Or you can do both, send to friends AND post publicly.

Private Snaps sent directly to friends can only be viewed twice, maximum. Unopened Snaps can sit in your friend's box for 30 days before it is automatically deleted. You can set how long a Snap can be viewed, up to 10 seconds.

As you get into a private Chat with friends, a lot more options open -- Voice, Video, Text, Stickers, etc. -- and we'll get more into that as we walk you through the process.

Public Snaps posted to Stories can only be seen by friends and followers. They can be viewed an unlimited number of times during 24 hours from posting.

You can also adjust who can and cannot see your Snaps and Stories in your Settings, which is accessible via the gear icon on your Profile.


## ALL THIS DISAPPEARS, SO I CAN SEND ANYTHING I WANT, RIGHT?

Um, no. Snaps sent to friends can only be viewed for up to 10 seconds once, or twice if the viewer immediately taps the Snap again -- but friends cannot watch the Snap a second time later if they have already moved on to another Snap.

Snaps in Stories, which is more public-facing since anyone following you can see those, can be viewed unlimited times within the 24 hours they are posted.

But viewers can ALWAYS take a picture of your Snap, so exhibit extreme caution with what you send out there. You the sender will be alerted when the viewer takes a screen capture directly from their phone, but viewers can always enlist tricks such as taking a shot of your Snap on their main phone from a second phone, for which you would not be alerted.

So as with any communications platform, please exhibit caution when deciding what to post.


## HOW DO I DELETE SNAPS?

There is no way to un-send a Snap sent via Chat; if you have sent someone a private Snap that you do not want the recipient to see, then you must delete your Snapchat account so that the Snap disappears before they open it.

And by cancelling your account, we mean cancel your account by notifying Snapchat, not just deleting the app off your phone (which doesn't actually cancel your account).

HOWEVER, to delete a Snap from your public Story, simply tap MY STORY in DISCOVER, open the individual Snap, then tap the garbage can icon.

And now that Snapchat has added MEMORIES, you can delete saved Snaps.

## CAN I ADD OUTSIDE / SAVED IMAGES TO MY SNAPS?

YES. Snapchat just added Memories in July 2016, which allows you to post Snaps using images accessed from your phone's camera roll.

However, Snaps made from saved images have a white border and are time-stamped in order to distinguish them from live Snaps.

Prior to this, you could only post Snaps using live pics and video.

Also, you can Faceswap with images from your phone's camera roll, and or send pics from your photo library to a friend via Chat.


## CAN I ADD HYPERLINKS TO MY SNAPS?

No, you cannot add live links to Snaps. You CAN type a URL in a Snap and encourage friends to capture the URL Snap's image, which they can then type into a browser themselves outside of Snapchat.

AND you CAN send a hyperlink to your friends directly in a Chat.


## HOW DO I FIND MY FRIENDS ON SNAPCHAT?

When you set up your profile, Snapchat asks to access your Contacts, so that it may find other Snapchat users in your phone's address book.

You can also add new users by 1) typing in / looking up names, 2) using Snapchat's Add Nearby, or 3) scanning Snapcodes -- all of which will be described in greater detail later.

## HOW CAN I TELL WHO HAS VIEWED MY SNAPS?

When you send a Snap, colored icons indicate who has opened / received / screeenshot / replayed your Snap -- see a list of these icons at http://bit.ly/snapicons

.

If you are posting Snaps to your public Stories, simply open Stories, tap the 3 dots to the right of My Story. Each Snap will be listed; next to each Snap will be the number of views that Snap received. Tap the numbered eyeball icon to see which your friends viewed your Snap.

## HOW DO I FIND PUBLIC FIGURES ON SNAPCHAT?

Simply type in famous names or brands under ADD FRIENDS in your Profile, or go to Snapcodes and sort through categories of popular subjects. http://bit.ly/snapcodes

As of this writing, Snapchat is starting to roll out more direct ways to connect with celebrities, mainly by tapping the celbrity's name when they are featured in Live Stories.

And depending on their settings, the two of you can Chat if they follow you back, or you may reply to Snaps they post in Stories.

## CAN I VIEW OTHERS' SNAPS WITHOUT FOLLOWING THEM?

You cannot -- the only way to view someone's Snap is to add them to your Friends list.

If you wish to unfollow them later, simply go to My Friends in your Profile, tap their Name, tap Settings (gear icon), tap Remove Friend.

## WHAT DO FRIENDS SEE WHEN THEY FOLLOW ME?

It all depends on your settings, but as new people join Snapchat and want to be your friend, the only thing they will see are Snaps which you post to your Story.

If you add them back to your Friends list, then the two of you can send each other Snaps via Chat.

## HOW DO I BLOCK PEOPLE FROM FOLLOWING ME?

All this is covered in greater detail later, but just so you know: Go to your PROFILE, tap ADDED ME or MY FRIENDS, tap that person's name, tap the Settings gear icon in the upper right of their Profile, then tap IGNORE or BLOCK.

## CAN I ADD PRIVATE GROUPS TO SNAPCHAT?

Not yet, but since so many people ask, this will likely come soon.

However, Snapchat automatically lists the friends with whom you Chat the most in the top of My Friends.

But to easily access a larger number of friends to send a private, direct Snap as a group, add a symbol or letter to the front of their name, like * or a, so they appear at the top of My Friends.

## HOW DO I GAIN FOLLOWERS?

Rule #1: tell your friends! Your Snapcode is your Snapchat ID that others can scan to add you; also share your ID's username or URL, like you would any regular web link (in email, other platforms, etc.).

Since Snapchat is primarily a chat app, a good portion of your initial Snapchat followers will come from your pre-existing network. But the more often you publish your Snapcode, your username, and your URL, the more people will find and follow you.

As Snapchat becomes more of a publishing destination, you may gain followers via traditional user acquisition / growth hacking tactics that you would use to build a base on other social networks.

## HOW DO I GET A *TON* OF PEOPLE TO FOLLOW ME?

There are more advance strategies to boost your follower counts (hiring influencers for Story takeovers, creating calls to action that lead back to your site, buying ads on other platforms, etc.), but we'll leave those for another book-- for right now, we just want to get you off the training wheels.

First, start with people you know, so you have friends and family with which to Chat.

Next, build compelling Stories, so that strangers have a reason to follow you or your brand.

Be INTERESTING, so that people want to come back to your Stories on a regular basis.

Be CONSTANT with your posts, so that people have something to come back to on a regular basis (a couple times a day is fine).

Be GENUINE with your posts -- if you're not a 14 year old kid, don't act like one. Sure, wacky characters get a lot of followers among The Kids, but if you are an expert on botany, interior design, or venture capital, you can build a highly-engaged niche audience, much like you would for your blog or website.

ENGAGE with your followers when they post replies to your Stories, if you have the time and energy. This can also be a good way to generate new business leads.

Post your SnapCode, username, and URL anywhere you would post your website's link, your email address, your LinkedIn addy, etc. -- eventually more adults will pick up on Snapchat, and they'll know how to find you when they do.

## HOW MANY SNAPS SHOULD I POST IN A DAY?

Brevity is the essence of power on Snapchat -- some celebrities may post dozens of Snaps to their Stories all day long in order to be on top of the Recent Updates list.

Maybe they actually do have something interesting to say, but I have to be honest -- I have a realllllly short attention span, and find myself going "tap tap tap" to skip next next next, or swiping down to get out of a Story if it's not holding my attention.

With that said, most experts recommend no more than 10 Snaps per 24 hours, unless you have something truly compelling to show & tell.

## CAN I TAKE SNAPS ALL DAY?

Sure, if you like -- just be aware that Snapchat uses a lot of bandwidth and battery life, so you will quickly burn data and burn your battery power by staying on Snapchat all day.

And although it's nice to capture and share the good times, sometimes it's better to just enjoy the moment and let it pass in real life.

## HOW DO I MAKE MY OWN GEOFILTERS?

There are online resources for photoshop mavens to build your own Geofilters, but for the rest of us, it is best to hire an experienced designer to build a Geofilter for your location or event, which is subject to Snapchat's approval and rates. http://bit.ly/snapgf

## WHERE CAN I LEARN MORE ADVANCED PRACTICES?

Snapchat is adding new features all the time. To learn more about these, or to get an even deeper knowledge on what you have already learned, go to http://bit.ly/snapchatsupport

There are a *lot* more tricks to learn well beyond the basics. But the point of this book is to get you well-versed on the baby steps in a short amount of time, without overwhelming you with too much information too soon.

# 3. SNAPCHAT TERMINOLOGY

**CAPTION** is the markup you make to a Snap. These can be done with Stickers, Text, or Doodles. [Image 2]

**CAPTURE** is the big round button in your camera that you use to start a Snap. Capture / Snap mode is also the default start page whenever you open Snapchat. [Image 1]

**CHAT** is the primary function of Snapchat, in which you can converse directly, privately with friends via Snaps, Stickers, video, voice, or text. [Image 6]

**DISCOVER** is the Snapchat newsstand, in which publishing partner channels such as CNN and Cosmopolitan deliver handcrafted Stories; these may be still images, animations, videos, or long-form text. [Image 5]

**DOODLE** is any drawing you do to a Snap. Access Doodle by tapping the pencil icon in the upper right of your Snapchat camera. [Image 2]

**FACE SWAP** is a feature within Lenses, which lets you swap your face with friends (or other properties which feature a face, like a statue, a poster, or your dog. Or a goat.).

**FILTERS / GEOFILTERS** are layers you can add on top of your Snaps to change color / tone, add time, temp, location, and speed; video filters include slow motion, fast-forward, reverse. [Image 2]

**IMAGE 1:** CAPTURE / SNAP mode, the first thing you see every time you open Snapchat, marked by the big CAPTURE button in the center bottom.

**IMAGE 2:** This SNAP was CAPTIONed with DOODLES, (GEO)FILTERS, STICKERS, and text.

**IMAGE 3:** This SNAP was made using one of many LENSES offered (FACESWAP is also in this batch).

18

**IMAGE 4:** Your PROFILE features your SNAP CODE, your SCORE, TROPHY CASE, and Friends list.

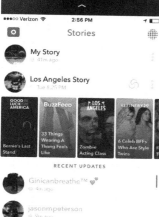

**IMAGE 5:** STORIES features DISCOVER from partners like ESPN and Buzzfeed; LIVE STORIES are built from users' SNAPS, and Recent Updates lists Friends' publicly-posted Stories.

**IMAGE 6:** CHAT is where you communicate privately via text, pics, Snaps, video, or voice with your friends.

**LENSES** are animated Filters that lie over your face for special selfies. Lenses can be accessed by putting your Snapchat camera in selfie mode, then pressing & holding your face. A grid then builds over your face, and Lense options magically appear. [Image 3]

**LIVE** is part of Stories, is where Snapchat builds stories from user-generated content based on location and current events. [Image 5]

**MEMORIES** is the feature which allows you to save your Snaps in-app or pull old / saved pictures from your phone's camera roll, thus enabling you to view or repost old Snaps or pictures. (Chapter 9)

**MODE:** There are only three modes of interaction in Snapchat: 1) SNAP (a/k/a Capture), which is signified by the camera interface you see every time you open Snapchat; 2) CHAT, which is signified by your Friends list; and 3) STORIES, which is signified by the newsstand and list of recent updates.

**REPLAY:** You / friends are allowed to immediately replay any just-viewed Snap in Chat one additional time by tapping that last Snap; you can not go back to that Snap later to replay.

However, you CAN replay Snaps within public Stories as many times as you like within 24 hours of its posting.

**SCORE** is a number Snapchat gives you based on your interactions (Snaps sent & received, Stories posted, etc.) -- important for kids, notsomuch for adults. But this may come into play as others judge you on your expertise. [Image 4]

**SNAP** is a single picture or video you have made to send privately to friends via Chat (which can only be viewed once + replayed once, and then disappears), or post publicly to your followers via Stories (which disappears 24 hours after posting). A Snap can be marked up with Text, Stickers, Doodles, and Filters. [Images 1, 2, 3]

**SNAPCODE** is your Snapchat ID, a yellow box filled with your Profile pic + a unique dot-code. Other users can follow you simply by hovering their Snapchat camera over your Snapcode and pressing your Snapcode for a couple seconds. [Image 4]

**SNAP STREAK** is when you and a friend have Snapped to each other for more than one consecutive day, designated by a flame next to your friend's name + a number next to the flame (to designate the Streak's total days) -- it's a source of pride for some users to see how long they can keep their Streaks going.

**STICKERS** are the emojis and images that you can layer over your Snaps. [Image 2]

**STORY** is a series of Snaps which have been stitched together over a 24-hour period. [Image 5]

**TROPHY CASE**, accessed via your Profile page, features all the trophies for all your Snapchat accomplishments -- again, important for kids, notsomuch for adults. [Image 4]

# Okay, let's get started!!!!

# 4. FIRST STEPS: GETTING STARTED

When you first hop on to Snapchat, you are going to receive a lot of prompts for the various features.

Keep in mind that for your first time on, all you really need to do is **connect with friends and send them a Snap**.

Everything else -- adding Text, Stickers, Doodles, Filters, shooting video, etc. -- is explained in greater detail in subsequent chapters. Soooo....

Go to the App Store to download the app

Snapchat will then prompt you to **SIGN UP**

Enter your **EMAIL ADDRESS**, your **NAME**, your **BIRTHDAY** (for age verification), a **USERNAME**, and your **PHONE NUMBER** for account verification

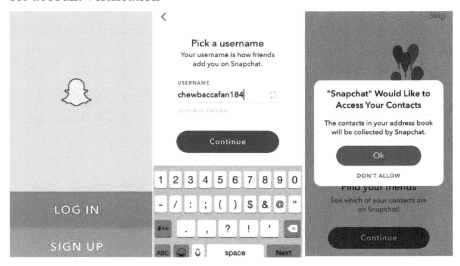

The app will then ask if it can **ACCESS YOUR CONTACTS** in order to find friends already on Snapchat.

This is important, because in order to make the best use of Snapchat, sending Snaps to friends, you should pick some friends to get started.

Snapchat will search your contacts to see who already uses the app -- tap the names of those friends already on Snapchat in order to start.

Those friends will get an alert that you are now following them, and they may in turn friend you on Snapchat based on such notifications.

Snapchat will then prompt you to **INVITE CONTACTS**, so that those not already on Snapchat receive an invite via mobile phone.

## NOW, GET READY FOR YOUR BIG MOMENT!

After these steps, Snapchat turns on your camera so you can take a picture of yourself! You also get a prompt to press the **CAPTURE** button, that big round button on the bottom of your screen.

After you press the Capture button, Snapchat will ask if you would like to use your location.

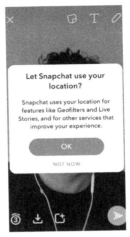

(I recommend allowing this, so that you can add Geofilters to your Snaps, and to access local Stories. (More on Geofilters & local Stories later.))

Next, Snapchat prompts you to add text. You can tap & hold the text to move / adjust it if you want, but let's keep it simple for right now.

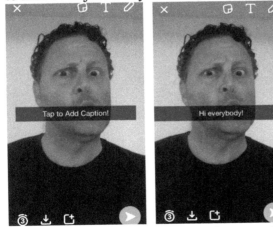

Press that big blue button in the bottom right, which then opens your friends list.

Pick the friends to which you would like to send your Snap, press the arrow bar at the bottom of the screen, and **JUST LIKE THAT, YOU HAVE SENT YOUR FIRST SNAP!**

**Keep in mind that every time you open Snapchat, the first thing you see is SNAP MODE.**

## And from SNAP MODE, you can do THREE THINGS:

**SNAP** (big lower middle circle) a picture or video, and send privately to friends (Chat) or publicly to followers (Stories)

**CHAT** (lower left circle) with friends, using Text, Images, Doodles, Stickers, Voice, and Video

**WATCH** (lower right circle) what others have publicly posted to Stories

# We will get into more detail on each icon in subsequent chapters, but just so you know:

**UPPER LEFT** = FLASH tap to turn flash on or off

**TOP MIDDLE** (Ghost icon) = **YOUR PROFILE** (Chapter 6)

**UPPER RIGHT** = CAMERA DIRECTION. tap to switch to your outward-facing camera, tap again to use your selfie camera. You can also double-tap your screen to switch front & back cameras.

**LOWER LEFT** = **CHAT**, this is where direct messages from friends and others show up. (Chapter 7)

**LOWER MIDDLE (BIG CIRCLE)** = **CAPTURE**, tap to take a picture, press and hold to make a video. (Chapter 5)

**LOWER MIDDLE (LITTLE CIRCLE)** = **MEMORIES**, tap to access saved Snaps or your phone's camera roll. **(Chapter 9)**

**LOWER RIGHT** = **STORIES**, tap this to see Stories posted by people you follow, or from branded publishers like CNN, Wall Street Journal, Comedy Central, etc. (Chapter 8)

# Now, let's get a better understanding of SNAPS, CHATS, and STORIES

# 5. HOW TO TAKE & SEND A SNAP

Simply open the app, or go back to Snap -- you know, that camera page with the Capture button.

From the last chapter, we learned:

**UPPER LEFT:** Press FLASH to turn Flash off or on.

**UPPER RIGHT:** Press CAMERA to have the camera face towards or away from you.

**MIDDLE BOTTOM:** Press big CAPTURE button to take a picture; hold to make a video.

## JUST LIKE THAT, YOU HAVE TAKEN A SNAP!

After you take a Snap, those symbols in the corners all change:

**UPPER LEFT** = X, tap to DELETE that Snap and go back to Snap mode (note: deleted Snaps cannot be retrieved).

**UPPER RIGHT** = the following options:

**PAPER** = **STICKERS**, where you can add a plethora of emojis to your Snap.

SWIPE and SCROLL through the stickers to find a wide array of options, from smiley faces to animals to hand signals, from hearts and flags to tiny people, food, and symbols of all sorts.

Take a moment and scroll through these, just to familiarize yourself with all the options.

If you TAP any of these Stickers, they show up on your Snap.

You can then pinch to enlarge / shrink your Sticker, rotate, or move these images anywhere on your Snap with you fingertips.

To DELETE any of these emojis, press & drag them up to the STICKERS icon, which then turns into a trash can.

## PRO TIP -- ANIMATED STICKERS:

If you snap a video, you can actually add a sticker and animate it to move along with any moving image simply by holding the sticker over the moving image you wish to stick it to -- magic!

**T = TEXT**, where you type in a message to caption the image.

Tap the T once, you get a message box to type into.

Tap the T again for larger text; tap again for large text centered.

A color bar also appears to the right, which allows you to change the text color.

Tap & hold the text to drag it anywhere you like, or pinch the text to expand or rotate it.

To DELETE / EDIT text, simply tap the text and use your keyboard.

**PENCIL = DOODLE**; when you tap this, a color bar appears in the upper right.

Simply tap a color of your choice and use your finger as a pencil to Doodle on your Snap.

To ERASE the Doodle, tap the curved arrow in the upper right until you've erased what you wanted.

To exit Doodle, press the arrow in the upper left.

## ADDING FILTERS FOR STILL PICTURES:

Swipe your image (left or right) to add a FILTER -- these include location tags, sponsored images, sepia tones, time, temperature (tap to change from Farenheit to Celcius), and speed (please, do not use Snapchat while driving).

## PRO TIP -- TWO FILTERS FOR STILL PICTURES:

Swipe left or right to add a FILTER. When you have chosen one Filter, press & hold your image, then continue swiping until you find a second Filter that you like. Voila!

## EXTRA FILTERS FOR VIDEO:

In addition to the above FILTERS, you can SLOW DOWN, SPEED UP, and REVERSE your video snap by choosing the snail, rabbit, fast rabbit, or rewind icons.

To DELETE a Filter, simply swipe the screen until the Filter no longer appears on your Snap.

## LOWER LEFT

**CLOCK = TIMER.** Tap this to adjust the amount of time in which you would like for your still image to appear, from 1-10 seconds.

**DOWNLOAD = SAVE.** Tap this to save your Snap to your phone's camera library. This comes in handy when you want to post your Snap to another social network.

**PAPER+ = ADD.** Tap this to add this Snap to your Story. Your Story is made up of a series of the Snaps you have publicly posted within the past 24 hours.

Your Story is viewable by any of your friends during that 24 hour period, unlike direct Snaps, which disappear after they have been viewed once in Chat (or twice -- more on this later).

If you have enabled Geolocation, you may also have the option to add a Snap to your area's Story. Since I live in LA and have Geolocation enabled, some of my Snaps which I have submitted to Snapchat's LA Story have actually made it onto the Snapchat Live's LA Story! More on this in the STORIES chapter.

## LOWER RIGHT

**ARROW = POST.** From here you get to decide where you wish to post your snap. Do you send it directly to friends? Or would you like to add it to your Story? Do you want to save your Snap to My Memories? Simply tap the boxes for those you wish to see it, and then it is automatically added or sent.

# OKAY OKAY, LET'S GET TO
# THE IMPORTANT STUFF:
# HOW DO I FACESWAP!

Let's get to one of Snapchat's coolest features, **LENSES,** where you can add those cool animations to your face, and yes, even Faceswap.

First, make sure your selfie camera is on during Snap mode.

Next, TAP AND HOLD YOUR FACE. Yep, your face.

A textured grid will then show up on your face, which tells Snapchat where to best stitch these masks, as a still or moving image.

Once Snapchat has scanned your face, LENSE options will appear across the bottom of your screen. As you swipe each option, that LENSE will appear on your face.

Simply pick the LENSE that best fits your mood -- dog, cat, panda, squishy face, cop (Lenses change daily), and yes, Faceswap.

A lot of the Lenses will prompt you to raise your eyebrows or open your mouth for full effect -- go ahead, give it a try!

**Once you find a Lense you like, press the round Capture button to Snap a picture; press & hold Capture to Snap a video.**

You can then enhance your Snap with Doodles, Stickers, Text, or Filters.

To FACESWAP, simply swipe left to one of the two two-circle options at the end of Lense options.

One two-circle option lets you Faceswap with a live partner next to you (a friend, a stranger, an animal, statue, a picture of Matt Damon, whatever it may be), and viola! Faces swapped. Move your face to adjust.

The second two-circle option let you Faceswap with a picture stored on your phone; choose that Lense option, then pick the picture that Snapchat pulls from your phone's library.

And like all Snaps, you can send these directly to friends via Chat, post as part of a Story, and / or save to Memories.

# 6. HOW TO SET UP YOUR PROFILE

When you are in SNAP mode (Snapchat's default / camera mode), tap the Ghost icon in the top middle.

This leads to your Profile, where you find your Snapcode, your Score, and your Trophy Case, and where you find / add friends.

**The first time you access your profile, Snapchat will prompt you to take a selfie for your Snapcode,** which will then appear in that dotted yellow box in the center.

When you tap the Capture button to set your Profile picture within your Snapcode, you will get a countdown clock, which, like a photo booth, will take five quick shots of you. Go ahead, make funny faces!

And if you don't like your Snapcode pics, you can always do-over and take new shots simply by pressing the big round button again.

Your Snapcode is used to identify yourself on Snapchat.

The dots in your Snapcode are unique to your ID, and makes it easy for other to follow you by simply hovering and tapping their Snapchat camera over your Snapcode.

Once you have taken your Snapcode selfie, there is an UPLOAD button in the upper right, which lets you save / share your Snapcode with others, so they may easily find and add you to their Snapchat.

## UPPER LEFT = QUESTION MARK

This shows you how to add friends via Snapcode (place your phone over their Snapcode, press and hold their Snapcode, and they are added). To get out of this, simply tap the screen.

## UPPER RIGHT = SETTINGS GEAR

This is where you adjust or manage your account settings -- Name, Username, Birthday, contact info, notifications, etc.

Halfway down Settings is the MANAGE tab, and this is very important -- this area lets you manage Filters, Travel Mode (data usage), Friend Emojis (cool for kids, not as important for most adults), and Phone Permissions.

You can also set up who can Send You Snaps and View Your Story -- Everyone, My Friends, Custom.

There is also a SNAPCASH tab, where you can pay friends on Snapchat via Snapchat. It's not a crucial function just yet, but be aware that it is an option.

To get out of Settings, tap the arrow in the upper left.

## UPPER MIDDLE = TROPHY CASE

This is where you unlock trophies for all your various activities, tap the icons to see which trophies you have won -- cool for kids, not as important for most adults.

**SNAPCODE:** This, the big yellow dotted box, is the code people use to add you simply by pressing & holding the Capture button with their Snapchat camera over your image.

Beneath that is your name, your username, as well as your Score (another abitrary measure Snapchat awards based on your

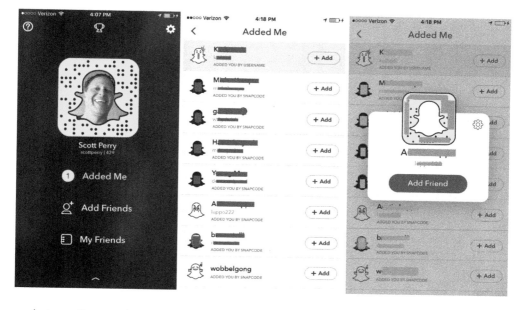

interactions -- important for kids, notsomuch for adults. But this may come into play as others judge you on your expertise.); these pieces are also visible when others open their My Friends list.

**ADDED ME:** This shows you who has recently added you as a friend, as well as how they added you (by Snapcode, by UserName, Phone Number, Added You Back, etc.)

**To ADD,** tap +ADD

**To EDIT NAME, IGNORE, or BLOCK,** tap their name, tap the Settings gear icon to the right, then tap the option you wish to choose.

**To get out of Added Me, tap the arrow in the upper left.**

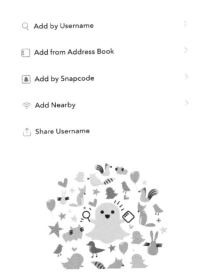

**ADD FRIENDS:** Tap this to add friends through a number of ways:

**BY USERNAME:** Type in their username, tap add.

**FROM ADDRESS BOOK:** Searches address book to add friends.

**BY SNAPCODE:** This accesses your photo library in case you shot a Snapcode when you saw a Snapcode but may have had limited internet access

**ADD NEARBY:** To add a friend, ask them to open Add Nearby, then tap the + next to their name.

**SHARE USERNAME:** Tap this for a message to pop up, in order to share your username via text or other socials.

**To get out of Add Friends, tap the arrow in the upper left.**

**MY FRIENDS:** This is your Snapchat address book, and it shows you the friends you have already added to Snapchat.

Your best friends, the ones you chat with the most, will appear at the very top of this list. Everybody else will be listed alphabetically by first name.

Next to some friends are emojis; the more you interact, the more the emojis change to reflect that level of interaction.

This is not important for everyone to know initially, so rather than overwhelm you with too much info, simply go here to see Emoji definitions + how to change friend's Emojis: http://bit.ly/scemojis

When you tap a Friend's name, their Profile appears. From here, you can tap their name to initiate a Chat or send them a Snap.

From their Profile, you can also tap that settings / gear icon to Edit their name (if you prefer to call them Honeypie or Farty McFartface), Remove Friend, or Block.

**To get out of My Friends, tap the arrow in the upper left.**

# To exit your Profile, swipe UP

# 7. HOW TO CHAT

When you open CHAT (lower left box in Snap mode), a record of all your recent Chats can be seen -- this shows in reverse chronology with whom you have Chatted and when.

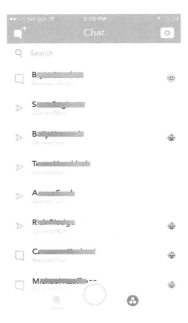

To the LEFT of each name is an icon that signifies the type of interaction -- find these definitions at http://bit.ly/snapicons

To the RIGHT of each name is an emoji that describes the level of interaction with that friend -- definitions at http://bit.ly/scemojis

[Note: These emojis & icons are nice to know, but not essential when getting started -- there's already enough details to pick up from this handbook, hence the links to these.]

**TO ENGAGE IN A CHAT**, simply find a Friend via the Search bar up top (or in the Chat list below) and swipe right. To send a quick Snap, doubletap that Friend's name and Snap mode opens.

**TIP:** To initiate a Chat with a friend directly from Snap mode, simply take a Snap, tap the arrow in the bottom right, and tap the friend(s) to whom you would like to send your Snap.

After opening the Chat window with another user, you will notice a ton more options than were available in Snap mode -- you can:

* Type a simple text

* Send a stored picture from your phone's camera roll

* Call friends directly via Voice Chat, or press & hold to leave a 10-second voice message

\* Send a Snap

\* Connect via Video Chat, or press & hold to leave a 10-second video message

\* Send an emoji Sticker.

The best thing about Chat is that you can perform all these functions from one base -- you might initiate a chat with a simple text, then send a funny picture or a Snap.

Mix up your Chat by adding a 10-second audio or video note, or even flip your phone's cameras while in video chat to show your friends what's going on around you!

**PRO TIP:** If you type a word such as "happy" or "hungry" before you tap the Sticker icon, emojis pertaining to that word appear first -- try it!

# YES, IT REALLY IS THAT EASY.

Once everyone in the Chat has viewed & closed the message, the message disappears from chat.

HOWEVER -- even though Chats disappear, they CAN be saved simply by pressing and holding the Chat (saved Chats are highlighted gray -- press & hold again to unsave. And to view saved chats, swipe down on your friend's open chat window).

And even though Chats cannot be shared with others, be aware that it is not difficult to take a screenshot of Snap, so as with any correspondence, exercise caution when deciding what to send.

# To exit Chat, simply swipe LEFT

# 8. VIEWING STORIES / DISCOVER

**STORIES** is where you see public Stories on Snapchat, either from Snapchat's publishing partners (**Discover**), Snapchat's internal team (**Live**), or from Friends (**Recent Updates**).

To access STORIES, click on the lower right button in SNAP mode.

When you go into STORIES, you see a wide array of options:

In the Upper Left, the camera icon takes you back to SNAP mode.

In the Upper Right, that globe of circles takes you to DISCOVER, Snapchat's news stand of publishing partners' Stories.

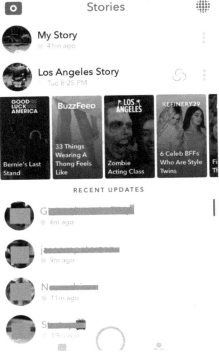

**MY STORY** sits at the top of Stories; from here you can review your most recent Story from the past 24 hours, delete Snaps within your Story, and see who has viewed your Story.

# HOW TO SEE WHO HAS VIEWED YOUR STORY

**TAP** the three vertical dots on the right of **MY STORY**.

This will then open a listing of each Snap within your Story; the number of views each Snap has received is displayed on the right.

TAP the eye icons to see who viewed that Snap within your Story.

**(TIP:** Press the Circled Arrow to save your Story to your phone.)

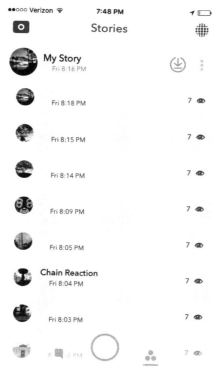

You will also see four buttons across the top:

**EYE** = Number of Views

**ARROWS** = How many / who has Screen Captured your Snap (more: http://bit.ly/snapicons)

**TRASH CAN** = Delete Snap

**DOWN ARROW** = Save Snap to your phone's camera library

## To get out of this mode, swipe DOWN

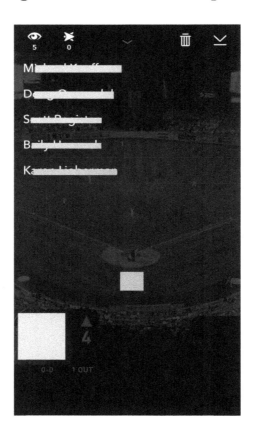

# DISCOVERING 'DISCOVER'

**DISCOVER** is Snapchat's news stand, where publishing partners post articles to their own branded Channels on a daily basis, whether they be still images, animations, videos, or long form text.

Tap a rectangle / cover to see what publishers are posting to their Discover channel, and see how pros tell their stories on Snapchat.

# HOW TO NAVIGATE STORIES INSIDE A DISCOVER CHANNEL:

To **READ** a Story within a Channel, SWIPE UP.

To **SKIP** a Story, SWIPE LEFT.

To **GO BACK** to a Story, SWIPE RIGHT.

To **SAVE** a Story, press & hold, add a Caption (Stickers, Doodles, Text) if you like, then tap the DOWNLOAD box in the Lower Left.

To **SHARE** a Story, press & hold, add a Caption if you like, tap the ARROW button in the Lower Right to send to a friend.

To **EXIT** a Channel, SWIPE DOWN.

Snapchat has also added a SUBSCRIBE button at the end of each article and Channel, making it easier for you to keep up with your favorite publishers.

# RECENT UPDATES =
# ALL YOUR FRIENDS' STORIES

Below Discover is **RECENT UPDATES**, in which the people you follow have their own Stories.

The most recently updated Stories appear at the top of that list, followed by All Stories, sorted alphabetically.

When you are viewing Stories, Snapchat automatically jumps to the next Story once the one you are viewing has wrapped -- so pay attention! (These may be separated by ads by the time you read this.)

And remember, Stories pulls together a user's public Snaps from the past 24 hours -- you can view Stories as many times as you like, but older Snaps in a Story do disappear after 24 hours.

To OPEN a STORY, tap the Friend's name.

To SKIP a SNAP within a Story, TAP the image.

To REPLY to a SNAP, SWIPE UP on that Snap to Chat (this option may be subject to the Friend's settings).

To SKIP a STORY and see the next Friend's Story, SWIPE LEFT.

To EXIT a STORY, SWIPE DOWN.

**To exit Stories, tap the camera icon in the Upper Left.**

# LIVE: BIG / LOCAL STORIES CURATED FROM USER POSTS

Below RECENT UPDATES is **LIVE**, where Snapchat's editorial team stitch together live Stories from big or geocentric events, curated from images + videos posted by Snapchat users on the scene.

Some Snaps may lead to even more Snaps around an event; **SWIPE UP** to Explore more.

To **SKIP** a Snap within a Story, tap the Snap or swipe left.

To **EXIT** a Story SWIPE DOWN.

# 9. NEW TO SNAPCHAT: MEMORIES

Just as we were to go to press in July 2016, Snapchat unleashed **MEMORIES** onto the world, allowing users to re-share old Snaps, as well as post Snaps using old pictures from your phone's camera roll.

This is a big deal, because prior to this, you were only allowed to post Snaps using live pictures & video taken directly within the app. And instead of saving your Snaps to your phone's camera roll, Memories saves your Snaps in-app, thus keeping you more engaged.

For the most part, users will store Snaps & Stories and show off these Memories while they hang out with friends in real life, as illustrated in Snapchat's own promo video. http://bit.ly/scmemories

But Memories also allows you to create new Snaps using pictures from your camera roll, as well as older Snaps, with one caveat -- said images have a white border and are time-stamped, so they look distinctly different from live Snaps.

Compare the live Snap (left) to one pulled from Memories (right)

To access Memories, tap the tiny circle at the bottom middle of SNAP.

When Memories opens, either Tap a saved Snap directly, or choose your library from the options listed across the top:

## ALL, SNAPS, STORIES, CAMERA ROLL, MY EYES ONLY

Once your chosen picture opens, you can either view it / show it to friends in real life, or repost it to Snapchat.

To repost to Snapchat, TAP image and SWIPE UP to Edit & Send.

Mark this image up with Stickers, Text, and Doodles if you like (review Chapter 5). Tap the arrow in the lower right to send your new Snap.

Snapchat then reverts back to that image; tap DONE in the upper left, Save or Discard your Snap, TAP & SWIPE DOWN to exit.

Notice an area in the upper left of your old Snap marked My Snap -- Tap that and three options appear:

**Export Snap**, which allows you to save that Snap to your camera roll or send it via other platforms (email, text, socials)

**Move to My Eyes Only**, which saves the Snap in a password protected area in-app (**note**: the first time you save a picture to My Eyes Only, you will be prompted to set up a 4-digit code that only you will know -- so choose wisely!)

**Create Story from this Snap**, which takes you back to Memories. From here, click on multiple Snaps to create a new Story which you can then send to friends or post to My Story.

**PRO TIP:** These options are also available when you tap the circled checkmark in the upper right of Memories, making them easily accessible via a row of icons that appear across the bottom.

**SEARCH:** And finally, if you click on the magnifying glass in the upper left of Memories, you can search Snaps by tags and subjects:

# 10. ADDITIONAL RESOURCES

Wow, can you believe it -- we're already at the end of the book!

Hopefully this handbook has been a great way for you to hop on to Snapchat fairly easily, and to get you used to all the basic functions of the app -- with a little practice, you will be a Pro in no time.

The best way to learn is by doing --

Play around in **SNAP** by taking pictures & videos, then mark them up with Captions & Filters, or even repost old Snaps via Memories.

Spend a half hour on **CHAT** with a friend, and play around with all the different audio / video / text / emoji functions.

Spend some time poking around **STORIES**; find & follow some influencers to see how they use Snapchat.

And when all else fails, **PAY A TEEN $50 TO SHOW YOU THE ROPES FOR AN HOUR.** Kidding.

To learn even more, you can always find tutorials and videos directly from Snapchat, accessible from the app or from your computer: http://bit.ly/snapchatsupport

The Support section of Snapchat is a wealth of information; but without the most basic basics detailed in this book, using the app can take a moment to get used to.

If you are looking for celebrities and brands to follow, we highly recommend the site Snapcodes: http://bit.ly/snapcodes

We will have tips & more at the following site, so be sure to sign up for email updates on Snapchat's latest features:

# HOWTOSNAPCHATBOOK.COM

While you're at it, go ahead and put these handy tips to use! Find your humble narrator by Snapping the Code below:

## So there you have it! Happy Snapping, Happy Chatting, enjoy the ride.

CPSIA information can be obtained
at www.ICGtesting.com
Printed in the USA
LVHW020001270520
656402LV00006B/497.